CHILDREN'S FAIRYTALE THEATRE

THREE PLAYS TO STAGE AND PERFORM

CINDERELLA

BEAUTY AND THE BEAST

ALADDIN

Terri Wiltshire

Heinemann

Children's Fairytale Theatre
was produced for Heinemann Children's Reference
by Cedarwood Press/Pinpoint Design.

First published in Great Britain in 1996 by Heinemann Children's Reference,
an imprint of Heinemann Educational Publishers,
Halley Court, Jordan Hill, Oxford, OX2 8EJ,
a division of Reed Educational & Professional Publishing Ltd.

MADRID ATHENS PARIS
FLORENCE PORTSMOUTH NH CHICAGO
SAO PAULO SINGAPORE TOKYO
MELBOURNE AUCKLAND IBADAN
GABORONE JOHANNESBURG KAMPALA NAIROBI

Editor: Joanna Swinnerton
Design: The Pinpoint Design Company
Photographer: Rex Caves
Illustrations by: Mike Walsh
Make-Up Artists: Isobel Staff & Julie Puddy
Costume: Rosemary Forsyth & Margaret Winters
Production Controller: Lorraine Stebbing

ISBN 0 600 58361 9 (HBK)
     0 600 58362 7 (PBK)

British Library Cataloguing-in-Publication Data.
A catalogue record for this book is available from
the British Library.

Printed in Italy

The publishers would like to thank the staff and children
of class three, St Leonards V & A School, Leighton Buzzard,
especially their teacher Mrs Nicholls and Headmistress
Mrs Price and also Truly Scrumptious model agency.

Also we gratefully acknowledge prop donations by Texas,
Leighton Buzzard/Dillamore, Leighton Buzzard, Sue Breen
and Bob Portway.

NOTE: Only use water-based face paints and make-up.
Children with sensitive skin should use all make-up and
face paint with caution.

Many of the photographs in this book show children
performing barefoot. Do not perform barefoot on wet,
dirty or otherwise dangerous surfaces.

CONTENTS

CINDERELLA

BEAUTY AND THE BEAST

ALADDIN

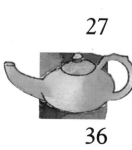

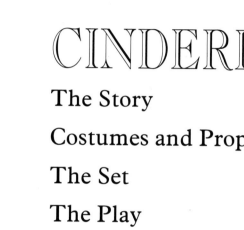

Welcome to the theatre! You may have seen a play before, and you may even have been in a play at school. But have you ever put on a play yourself? It takes a lot of time and work, but it's a lot of fun, too.

'But I don't like acting.'

Even if you don't like acting, there are lots of things you can do – you need more than actors to put on a play. Here are some of the things you can do.

The Director
Every play needs a DIRECTOR, who chooses and directs the actors and stage crew when they REHEARSE – this is when you practise the play.

The Stage Crew
The STAGE CREW help to prepare and put on the play. Here are some of the things the stage crew can make:

Each actor needs a COSTUME, and someone has to make these, and help the actors to put them on. They can also help the actors to put on their MAKE-UP.

The actors use PROPS on stage, such as wands and crowns; someone has to make these, and keep an eye on them during the play, to make sure they are ready when the actors need them.

You may need to make STAGE FURNITURE, like cupboards and tables, and someone has to move them on and off the stage during the play.

If your play has SOUND EFFECTS, such as the sound of a galloping horse, someone has to make those noises off-stage.

If you have LIGHTS and CURTAINS for your stage, someone must operate them at the right time.

A PROMPT sits backstage with a copy of the play, and if the actors forget their words, the prompt whispers the first word or two to help them.

MAKE-UP

Actors need make-up on stage, as they will look very pale without it. Use either theatrical water-based face paints, or ordinary make-up.

1 Spread some pink blusher on your cheeks on and under the cheekbone to make them rosy.

2 Cover your eyelids with light brown or blue eyeshadow. Brush your eyelashes with mascara.

3 Put some lipstick on your lips – and you're ready for the stage!

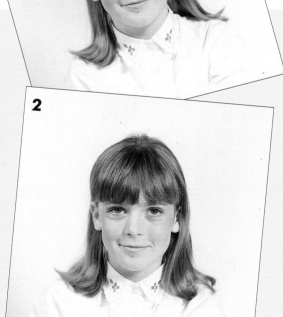

'How do we start?'

1. Decide which play you want to put on. There are three to choose from in this book. Each play has a CAST LIST, a list of all the people in the play. If you have too many actors, some of them can be EXTRAS. Extras appear on-stage but don't have any lines to say, such as party guests and palace guards.

2. Choose someone to be the director. The director tells the actors and stage crew what to do at the rehearsal.

3. Decide who is going to play which part. The director organizes an AUDITION, which is when everyone reads aloud parts of the play and agrees which they want to play.

4. The stage crew decide what they want to do. Look in the section for your play called Costumes and Props to see what costumes, props, stage furniture and sound effects you need.

5. Let your family and friends know you are putting on a play. You could make posters and tickets to tell people when and where it is. Make sure you show the name of the play and the day, time and place where it will be performed.

NEXT! The stage crew can begin to set up the THEATRE, and make the props and costumes.

READING A SCRIPT

Reading a SCRIPT is very different from reading an ordinary story. A script is made up of two parts:

● the actors' LINES. These are the words that each character says.

● the STAGE DIRECTIONS. These tell the actor when and where to enter (appear on the stage) and when to exit (leave the stage). They also tell you how to act when you say your lines. For example, if you're supposed to be angry, you could change your voice or wave your fist in the air.

Jim: Where are you going?
Tom: To the haunted house on Mill Street. Want to come?
Jim: *(looking frightened and shaking his head)* No!
Tom: *(laughing)* What's the matter? Chicken?
Jim EXITS LEFT, angrily.

Sometimes the stage directions will tell you to say your lines OFF-STAGE. This means you are hidden in the wings and the audience can hear you speak but they can't see you.

You must listen for your CUE so that you know when it is time to say your lines. A cue is what happens just before it is your turn to speak or move. It could be a sound, like someone screaming or a doorbell ringing, or it could be another actor's words, such as 'Here she comes'.

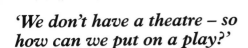

'We don't have a theatre – so how can we put on a play?'

The Theatre

You don't need a real theatre to put on a play. A theatre can be a patio, your garage, or your living room.

You need three main areas:
1. The STAGE – a place to act;
2. The WINGS – where the actors stand when they're not on-stage so that the audience can't see them;
3. The AUDITORIUM – where the audience sits.

The Stage

You can make a curtain to go across the front of the stage by draping an old sheet or blanket over a rope or clothes-line attached to something sturdy.

The Wings

These go either side of the stage. There are various ways of making wings. Stack cardboard boxes at the sides of the stage; or put up more curtains; or use ready-made screens if you have them.

The Auditorium

All you need is lots of chairs, and perhaps a row of cushions at the front, if some people don't mind sitting on the floor. Make sure that the chairs and cushions are placed so that everyone can see clearly.

Stage Furniture

Sometimes you can use the furniture from your home, and sometimes you can make it yourself. For example, for 'Cinderella', you will need a table and chairs, and a clock made out of cardboard boxes (see page 12).

Scenery

You may need some scenery for your stage. The easiest way to do this is to make some FLATS. To make flats, take several large sheets of cardboard and tape them together. Paint on them the scene that you want, such as bricks to show a stone wall, or trees to show a forest. Tape cardboard boxes against the back to make them stand up.

Props and Costumes

You may need a trumpet or magic wand, or a basket of fruit. You might find some of the props around your house, but if not, you can make them. Each play tells you what props you need and how to make them. If your character needs a special costume or make-up, make sure you try it out a day or two before the performance, so you can alter it if necessary.

Sound Effects, Lights and Curtains

The stage crew should read through the play to find out what sounds they need to make, and what they need to make them. They should also learn when the lights and curtains must be operated.

NEXT! The actors and stage crew practise what to do – this is called rehearsing.

'How do we learn what to say and do on the stage?'

1. At the first rehearsal, all the actors read the play aloud a few times to get used to the story and their lines. This is called a READ-THROUGH. Think about your character and how they should move and talk, and what expressions they have. Read the section on page 5 about how to read a script.

2. The director will tell you where to stand or sit or walk when you are on stage. Remember these STAGE DIRECTIONS and carry them out at each rehearsal.

3. The only way to learn your LINES is to practise, practise, practise! You can't learn all of your lines right away, so in the beginning you can read from the script.

4. Once you know your lines, practise several times without the script. The PROMPT will help you if you forget.

5. While the actors rehearse their lines, the STAGE CREW rehearse when to make the sound effects and when to operate lights and curtains.

6. Before the performance, have a DRESS REHEARSAL. This is when you perform the whole play with everything in place – props, sound effects, lights, make-up and costumes – to make sure that everyone knows what they're doing.

NEXT! It's time for the opening night!

Hints for Actors

1. Don't turn your back to the audience – they won't be able to hear you.

2. Always speak loudly and clearly, but don't shout.

3. Don't stand in front of other actors.

4. Don't talk when you are backstage, unless you are supposed to be saying a line off-stage.

5. If something goes wrong, and you forget your words or drop something, don't worry – keep going! Pretend it was meant to happen and carry on.

CINDERELLA
THE STORY

Before the first rehearsal, read through the script on your own so that you know the story. If you are acting a part, think about the character of the person you play and the best way of showing it.

Act 1

Cinderella is a servant to the bad-tempered Mrs Wormwood and her selfish daughters Whinella and Frumpella. The two sisters hate Cinderella, and they are always bullying her. One morning, the Prince's servant arrives with an invitation to a grand party at the palace. Cinderella longs to go, but the Wormwoods remind her of all the housework she must do. They laugh as they dress for the party.

Act 2

The Wormwoods leave for the party at the palace. Cinderella is very sad to be left behind and begins to cry. Then her Fairy Godmother appears, and with her magic wand she creates a golden coach. She turns Cinderella's rags into a beautiful dress and replaces her worn old shoes with glass slippers. As Cinderella leaves for the party, the Fairy Godmother warns her that she must be home before midnight.

MRS WORMWOOD
She always has a scowl on her face. She often has her arms crossed or her hands on her hips.

CINDERELLA
A gentle and patient girl. She never loses her temper or complains.

WHINELLA
She talks in a whiny voice and complains about everything.

CAST LIST

- ★ Cinderella
- ★ Mrs Wormwood
- ★ Whinella Wormwood
- ★ Frumpella Wormwood
- ★ The Fairy Godmother
- ★ The Prince
- ★ The Prince's Servant
- ★ Party guests – as many as you like
- ★ Palace guards

Act 3

At the palace, the Prince greets his party guests. Whinella and Frumpella push and shove to get his attention. But when he sees Cinderella, he ignores them and asks Cinderella to dance with him. They talk and dance all evening, and when the clock strikes twelve, Cinderella rushes out in a panic, leaving behind one of her glass slippers. The Prince is upset and vows to find her.

Act 4

The next morning, Cinderella sings happily as she works, and the sisters talk about the party. The Prince and his servant arrive and announce that the Prince will marry the girl whose foot fits the glass slipper. Frumpella and Whinella try on the slipper, but their feet are too big. Cinderella asks to try it on, and to everyone's amazement it fits. The Prince takes Cinderella's hand, and they all go off to prepare the wedding.

THE FAIRY GODMOTHER
She is still training and has to keep looking at her notes. She's afraid of mice.

FRUMPELLA
A bad-tempered girl. She often stamps her foot when she doesn't get her own way.

THE PRINCE
A kind and generous man. He always sees the good in people.

THE PRINCE'S SERVANT
She thinks she's better than everyone else because she works for the Prince.

CINDERELLA

She wears a party dress and old shoes under a long, tattered cape, and needs some glass slippers for going to the party. She also needs a bucket, a scrubbing brush and a broom. Make some glass slippers as shown and follow the instructions below to make the cape.

CINDERELLA'S GLASS SLIPPERS

1 Take two ready-made gift-wrap bows and paint them all over with thin glue.

2 Place them on newspaper and sprinkle glitter over them. Leave to dry.

3 Attach them to a pair of shoes with paper-clips.

WHINELLA and FRUMPELLA

Both wear long skirts and blouses, and put on fancy capes and jewellery when they go to the party. Make two short capes as shown and decorate them with shiny buttons to look like jewels.

CAPES

1 Take a piece of fabric large enough to wrap around you (about 1m wide). Cut small slits along the top edge about 7cm apart.

2 Weave a wide ribbon through the slits and draw it tight.

3 Drape the cape over your shoulder and tie the ribbon loosely around your neck.

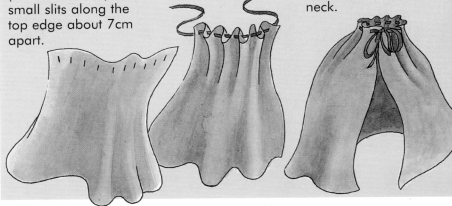

MRS WORMWOOD

She wears a long skirt and blouse. Follow the instructions above to make a cape for her to wear to the party, and decorate it as shown.

THE WORMWOODS' CAPE

Make a short cape and decorate it with shiny buttons or sequins.

CINDERELLA'S CAPE

Make a long cape that will hide Cinderella's party dress, and sew or glue on patches of different fabric so that it looks tattered.

THE FAIRY GODMOTHER'S CAPE

Make a short cape from black fabric and decorate it with gold stars cut out of foil or yellow felt.

THE PRINCE

The Prince wears trousers, a tunic and a crown. A long white shirt is perfect for the tunic. Sew gold buttons or braid down the front and on the shoulders. Make a crown, as shown.

THE PRINCE'S CROWN

1 Cut the crown shape from a piece of cardboard. It should be long enough to go round your head, with a bit to spare.

2 Glue or tape the ends together firmly and leave to dry.

3 Cover the crown in foil and decorate it with buttons, sweets or shapes cut out of coloured foil.

THE FAIRY GODMOTHER

She wears a short cape over a party dress and party shoes. She carries a magic wand and some pieces of paper that have her spells on. Make a magic wand as shown and follow the instructions on page 10 to make the cape.

FAIRY GODMOTHER'S WAND

1 Cut two star shapes out of cardboard. For the handle, use a stick or a long thin piece of cardboard.

2 Tape the handle to one of the stars. Glue the other star over it to hide the join.

3 Cover the wand with silver foil or paint it silver or gold.

THE PRINCE'S SERVANT

She wears trousers, a shirt, and a floppy hat with a feather. She needs a cushion, some glasses to read the invitation, and a scroll. To make the scroll, roll up a sheet of plain paper and tie it with a ribbon.

PALACE GUARDS

All the guards wear shirts, trousers and sashes across their chests, and they carry flags. To make a royal flag, cut a triangular piece of fabric and tape it to a mop handle. Paint a crown or a shield on the flag.

PARTY GUESTS

These can dress in their own party clothes, or wear costumes like the Prince's or the Wormwoods'.

ACTS ONE, TWO and FOUR

These take place in the Wormwoods' house.

- Place a table and some chairs on the stage.
- Stack dishes on the table.
- Place a bucket and scrubbing brush on the stage.

ACT THREE

This takes place in the ballroom of the palace. Set this scene in front of your curtain.

- Place a bench on the stage.
- Make a clock.

CLOCK

1 Take several cardboard boxes, stack them on top of one another and tape them together with brown tape. Make the bottom box larger than the others, so that the clock won't fall over.

2 Stick a circle of white paper on the front of the top box and paint on the face of a clock, with the hands at midnight.

3 Paint the front and the sides of the clock black.

SOUND EFFECTS

WHIP

To make the sound of a whip cracking, hold the ends of a leather belt and quickly pull it tight.

HORSES' HOOFS

To make the sound of horses' hoofs, tap two coconut halves together or on a wooden surface.

CHIMING CLOCK

To make the sound of a chiming clock, bang the lid of a large metal cooking pot with a big metal spoon.

THE PLAY
ACT ONE

The Wormwoods' house. Cinderella is scrubbing the floor and she stops to wipe her forehead. At that moment Frumpella and Whinella ENTER.

Frumpella: *(staring at Cinderella)* Did you see that? She wasn't doing her work.

Whinella: *(she points at Cinderella and calls in a whiny voice)* Mother, Mother. Cinderella wasn't doing her work.

Frumpella: You're in trouble now, Cinderella. Mother doesn't like lazy servants.

Whinella: *(shaking her head)* No she doesn't. And we caught you.

Frumpella: *(glaring at Whinella)* I caught her.

Whinella: Well, I was right behind you. I could have caught her.

Frumpella: *(pushing Whinella)* Could not.

Whinella: *(pushing back)* Could too.

Frumpella: *(louder)* Could not.

Mrs Wormwood ENTERS.

Mrs Wormwood: Frumpella! Whinella! Quiet.

The sisters are quiet but stick their tongues out behind their mother's back.

Mrs Wormwood: Now, what seems to be the problem?

Whinella: It's Cinderella. We caught her.

Frumpella: She wasn't working. She was just sitting there.

Mrs Wormwood: Not doing her work? Is this true, Cinderella?

Cinderella: No. I was just brushing the hair from my eyes.

Mrs Wormwood: Well, if you have so much time, we'll have to give you more work to keep you busy.

Frumpella: Oh, good. I have thirty-four dresses that need ironing.

Whinella: And I have sixty-two socks that need washing.

Mrs Wormwood: And I'd like my room painted again. Pink this time. And when you're finished with that....

(SOUND) There is a knock at the door. Mrs Wormwood looks at Cinderella.

Mrs Wormwood: Well? Answer the door.

Cinderella EXITS and we hear her and the servant off-stage.

Servant: *(off-stage)* Good day, Miss. I am a servant of the Prince. I am here to make a royal announcement.

Mrs Wormwood and her daughters look excited and clap their hands together.

Cinderella: *(off-stage)* Certainly. Come this way.

Cinderella ENTERS with the servant. Frumpella and Whinella curtsy and giggle. The servant puts on some glasses, unrolls a scroll and clears her throat.

Servant: The extremely handsome and unbelievably rich prince who lives in yon castle *(pointing off-stage)* invites all of his subjects to a grand party at the palace tonight.

She rolls up the scroll and EXITS, while the sisters squeal with excitement.

Frumpella: Mother, did you hear that?

Whinella: The prince. I'm going to meet the Prince.

Frumpella: I am too, you know.

Whinella: Not if I meet him first.

Frumpella: Will too!

Whinella: Will not!

Cinderella: He said all of his subjects. That means I can go!

Mrs Wormwood and her daughters look at one another and laugh.

Mrs Wormwood: Don't be silly. You have work to do. Now come upstairs and help us get dressed.

Frumpella: Cinderella meeting the Prince! The very idea!

They EXIT, laughing, and Cinderella follows them sadly.

ACT TWO

The Wormwoods' house. Cinderella ENTERS with a scrubbing brush and a bucket of water.

Frumpella & Whinella: *(off-stage)* Goodbye, Cinderella! Have fun with your cleaning! *(They laugh)*

(SOUND) The crack of a whip and horses' hoofs. Cinderella sits down, puts her head on the kitchen table and starts to cry. The Fairy Godmother ENTERS and moves around the stage as if she's searching for something.

Fairy: Excuse me. Have you seen a little piece of paper about this big? *(She measures with her fingers.)*

Cinderella: *(surprised)* Who are you?

Fairy: Your Fairy Godmother. Well, Fairy-Godmother-in-training, really. But I can't do very much without my notes.

Cinderella: What's that in your hand?

Fairy: *(looking at the notes in her hand with surprise)* Now I remember. I put them there so I wouldn't forget. Why am I here, exactly?

Cinderella: I don't know.

Fairy: You must know. Is there something you want?

Cinderella: Well, I would like to go to the Prince's party tonight.

Fairy: Is that all? Well, that's easy. I can whip up a fake invitation in no time. *(She waves her wand.)*

Cinderella:	I've already been invited.
Fairy:	Then what are you waiting for?
Cinderella:	I have all this work to do. (*She spreads her arms to show the dirty floors.*)
Fairy:	Oh, that's not a problem. I worked my way through Fairy School washing dishes. I'll have this place shining in no time. (*She starts to wave her wand again.*)
Cinderella:	But I have no way to get there. And besides, look at my clothes. They'll never let me in looking like this.
Fairy:	(*lowering her arms*) Hmm. You're right. Well, there's no getting around it. You'll have to find four (*she makes a face to show her disgust*) mice. And a nice fat pumpkin.
Cinderella:	Mice?
Fairy:	Oh, I'm sure they're very nice little creatures, but I was hoping to get by without them.
Cinderella:	And a pumpkin?
Fairy:	Yes! Yes! Now hurry up. Go outside and find them.

Cinderella EXITS and the Fairy Godmother practises her wand-waving.

Fairy: Inky-Binky-Zoo. No, that's not right.

Cinderella: *(off-stage)* Will this pumpkin do?

Fairy: *(looking off-stage through the door)* Perfect.

Cinderella: *(ENTERS and points off-stage)* And those mice?

Fairy: Yuck. Yes, I suppose so. Leave them out there. I don't want them running around my feet. Now hurry, Cinderella. We don't have much time. *(She leads Cinderella to the centre of the stage.)* Now turn around three times.

The Fairy Godmother raises her arms as she waves her wand so that her cape hides Cinderella from the audience. As Cinderella turns, she takes off her cape.

Fairy: Piffle-whiffle Kalamazoo!
Bunky-skunk, Ker-plunk, Ka-do.

When the Fairy Godmother stands aside, Cinderella is dressed in her party dress, but she is wearing her old shoes.

Fairy: *(proudly)* Well, what do you think?

Cinderella: It's beautiful, but what about –

Fairy: And don't forget your carriage.

The Fairy Godmother points off-stage, and Cinderella looks out of the door.

Cinderella: *(excitedly)* A golden carriage and four white horses. They're very nice, but – *(She points to her feet.)*

Fairy: Oh, my. Can't have that. They must be around here somewhere. *(She searches the stage for the glass slippers and finds them in Cinderella's bucket.)*

Fairy: Here they are. *(She taps the wand against her hand.)* I'm going to have to get this thing re-tuned.

Cinderella: Oh, thank you. They're beautiful. *(She puts them on.)*

Fairy: Hurry now. You don't want to be late.

She pushes Cinderella off-stage.

Cinderella: *(as she EXITS)* Thank you, Fairy Godmother.

Fairy: *(waving)* Have a good time. But make sure you're back by midnight. The magic disappears at midnight.

(SOUND) The crack of a whip and horses' hoofs.

CURTAIN

ACT THREE

At the palace there are crowds of party guests talking to one another. The Prince's servant is also on stage with the palace guards. Mrs Wormwood and her daughters are standing at the front.

Frumpella: I wish the Prince would arrive. How do I look?

Whinella: Not as good as I do.

Frumpella: I do too.

Whinella: Do not.

Frumpella: Do too.

Mrs Wormwood: Girls. Shh! The Prince!

The Prince and his servant ENTER. The servant claps her hands loudly.

Servant: Ladies and gentlemen. Prepare to meet His Royal Highness, the Prince.

Guests: *(clapping and bowing)* The Prince! Ah! Your Highness.

All of the girls hurry to be the first to meet the Prince. Frumpella and Whinella push and shove their way in. Cinderella ENTERS and steps to the end of the queue. The Prince starts at the beginning and shakes each girl's hand.

Prince: How do you do?

Girl: *(curtsying)* Your Majesty.

He repeats this with each girl. Frumpella and Whinella get excited as he gets closer. Just before he reaches them he sees Cinderella and goes to her.

Prince: Hello.

Cinderella: How do you do, your Majesty?

The Prince takes her by the hand and leads her to the bench. They sit and talk quietly.

Frumpella: *(angry)* Well, I never.

Whinella: *(whining)* Mother, he didn't even say hello.

Frumpella: Who is that girl? Who does she think she is?

Whinella: We were here first. It isn't fair.

The party guests dance and talk for a few minutes, to show that time is passing. Cinderella and the Prince are smiling and talking.

(SOUND) The clock strikes twelve and Cinderella stands up.

Cinderella: Oh no. It's late.

Prince: *(surprised)* We have plenty of time. It's only midnight.

Cinderella: Midnight? Oh dear. I have to go.

Prince: Please, you can't. I have so many more questions.

Cinderella: I'm sorry, but I must.

She EXITS and the Prince hurries after her and EXITS.

Prince: *(off-stage)* Please, wait! Come back!

The Prince ENTERS looking sad. He is holding one of Cinderella's glass slippers. He goes to his servant and hands her the slipper.

Prince: Prepare the royal carriage. Tomorrow we'll search the kingdom for the girl who wears this slipper.

The Prince EXITS and the servant calls after him.

Servant: But your Highness, there are so many other girls.

The other girls look unhappy and EXIT, complaining, followed by the boys.

Guests: *(Each girl says a different thing; they all talk at once.)*
It's not fair. I don't remember seeing her before. Who invited her?
I spent all my money on a new dress.

CURTAIN

ACT FOUR

The Wormwoods' house. Cinderella is in her tattered cape again, sweeping the floor. She hums happily to herself. Frumpella and Whinella ENTER.

Frumpella: If you hadn't stepped on my toe, you big oaf, and made me stumble, we would've been closer to him.

Whinella: Well, if you hadn't been combing your hair in the royal mirror, we wouldn't have been so late.

Frumpella: I just know if the Prince had seen us first, he'd never have noticed that simple little nobody.

Mrs Wormwood ENTERS, waving her arms.

Mrs Wormwood: *(excitedly)* Girls! Girls! The Prince is coming!

Frumpella & Whinella: *(squealing)* The Prince? Oh how do I look? Where's my brush? Do I have time to change?

The Prince and his servant ENTER. The servant is carrying a pillow with Cinderella's slipper sitting on top.

Servant: *(loudly)* His Majesty, his Royal Highness, the Prince who lives in yon castle –

Prince: Yes, yes. They know who I am. Don't make a fuss.

Servant: *(clearing her throat)* The Prince wishes it to be known that whoever can wear this slipper will be his wife.

Frumpella: Me first. I'm the oldest.

Whinella: No, me. I'm the prettiest.

They fight over the chair. Frumpella sits down first and the servant tries to put the slipper on her foot, but it won't fit.

Frumpella: My feet are just swollen. They swell up like pumpkins in the summer. Couldn't I try again in September?

Whinella: *(pulling her sister out of the chair)* My turn. She always did have big feet.

The servant tries the slipper on Whinella, but it won't fit.

Whinella:	I don't understand it. I've always had very dainty feet. Haven't I, Mother? Tell them.
Mrs Wormwood:	It's true. Couldn't you try one more time?
Cinderella:	*(stepping forward)* Could I try it on, please?

They all look at her in disbelief. The sisters giggle.

Mrs Wormwood:	Don't be silly, Cinderella. You're a nobody.
Cinderella:	*(to the Prince)* Please?
Servant:	Well, really, your Majesty. I think we should go.
Prince:	The young lady would like to try on the slipper.
Servant:	But look at her rags. Surely you can't be serious.
Prince:	I said all maidens in the kingdom and that includes this young lady.

He takes the shoe and helps Cinderella to sit in the chair. As he kneels to put it on her foot, the others crowd around to watch, blocking her from the audience. While she is hidden, Cinderella drops her cape to reveal her party dress.

Servant:	*(surprised)* It fits!
Whinella:	It must be a trick. I want a second chance.

They step back and Cinderella stands up. The Prince takes her hand and leads her to the centre of the stage.

Prince:	I knew it was you, even in rags.
Servant:	So does this mean . . .
Prince:	Yes, I've found my bride. We'd better get started with the preparations. Cinderella?

The Prince and Cinderella EXIT and the servant follows.

Frumpella:	I knew it was Cinderella, all along.

Mrs Wormwood and her daughters EXIT, talking as they go.

Whinella:	Did not.
Frumpella:	Did too.
Mrs Wormwood:	Girls! Girls!

CURTAIN

BEAUTY & THE BEAST

THE STORY

Before the first rehearsal, read through the script on your own so that you know the story. If you are acting a part, think about the character of the person you play and the best way of showing it.

Act 1

A kind merchant returns home after a long trip, bringing terrible news for his children Annette, John Paul and Beauty. He had picked a rose from a castle garden for Beauty, and as he did so, a huge beast appeared. It demanded that he pay for the rose by staying at the castle for ever. Annette and John Paul blame Beauty, and say that she should go instead. Sadly, she agrees.

Act 2

Beauty arrives at the beast's castle, and he shows her to her room. In it there is a magic mirror that will give Beauty anything she asks for, and in which she can see her family. The Beast brings Beauty gifts and asks her to marry him, but she always refuses. Beauty sees in the mirror that her father is very ill and begs to visit him. The beast agrees, but warns that he will die if Beauty is away for more than a week.

ANNETTE
Beauty's sister is spiteful and selfish. She bullies her brother into helping her.

THE MERCHANT
A good-hearted man who loves his children. He is very sad to lose Beauty, as she is his favourite.

DOCTOR
He or she comes to see the Merchant when he is ill.

BEAUTY
A kind and brave girl, who sees the best in everyone, even in her unkind brother and sister and the ugly beast.

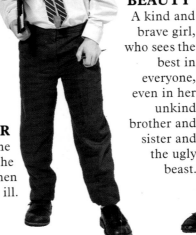

CAST LIST

- ★ Beauty
- ★ The Beast
- ★ A Doctor
- ★ Entertainers – clowns, musicians, dancers
- ★ The Merchant, Beauty's father
- ★ Annette, Beauty's sister
- ★ John Paul, Beauty's brother

Act 3

Beauty returns home and her father is overjoyed to see her. She promises to stay until he is well again, but then she must return. Annette and John Paul are jealous of the presents the Beast has given her, and they plot to keep her away from the castle for an extra day.

Act 4

When Beauty returns to the castle, she finds that the Beast is dying. She realises that she loves him after all, and tells him so. As he recovers, she sees that he is no longer a beast but a handsome prince. He explains that he was put under a spell, which could be broken only if a kind-hearted girl loved him. He asks her to marry him, and this time she says yes.

JOHN PAUL
Beauty's brother is weak and selfish. He pretends to be strong, but can't even stand up to his pushy sister.

THE BEAST
A huge creature, who growls and bellows and terrifies all who see him. He seems ferocious, but is shy and kind-hearted underneath.

ENTERTAINERS
They entertain Beauty in the castle. There can be as many clowns, musicians and dancers as you like.

THE MERCHANT
He wears knee breeches, a shirt, a waistcoat, and boots. Make the knee breeches as shown.

THE MERCHANT'S BREECHES

1 Take a pair of old trousers and cut off the legs below the knee.

2 Cut 5cm up the outside seam of each leg.

3 Make holes around the bottom edge of each leg, then thread a piece of ribbon through them. Tie in a bow.

JOHN PAUL
He wears knee breeches, boots, a shirt and a waistcoat. He also needs a duster to polish his boots. Make the waistcoat as shown, and follow the instructions above to make the knee breeches.

JOHN PAUL'S WAISTCOAT

1 Take a piece of felt that reaches from your neck to your waist, and goes once around you. Fold the edges into the middle.

2 Cut holes for the neck and arms. Sew or stick with fabric glue at the shoulders.

3 Cut slits for the buttonholes and sew on buttons. Decorate as shown.

BEAUTY
She wears a long skirt and blouse. She has a sash around her waist, tied in a bow at the back. Her clothes are very plain. She also needs a book, a suitcase and a handkerchief.

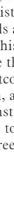

ANNETTE
Annette wears a long dress with a sash around the waist tied in a bow at the back. Annette is more dressed up than Beauty – she has ribbons in her hair and she wears jewellery. She also needs a box of chocolates.

THE BEAST

He wears a long fur robe and a mask. He also needs a pile of books, a tray of food with a napkin over it, a bunch of flowers, a necklace and a beautiful dress to give to Beauty. To make the robe, stick or sew some fake fur on to the edges of an old bathrobe. Make the mask as shown.

THE BEAST'S MASK

1 Blow up a balloon and smear one side with oil. Mix two spoonfuls of flour with eight spoonfuls of water. Dip strips of newspaper into this paste and place them on the greased side of the balloon.

2 When you have pasted on several layers, let it dry overnight then burst the balloon. Trim the edges to make a mask. Cut holes for the eyes, nose and mouth. Paint the mask brown.

3 When the paint is dry, punch a hole at each side and thread a piece of elastic through the holes.
Tie knots in the ends. Glue fake fur above the eyes and around the chin.

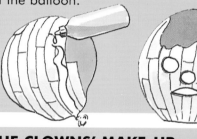

THE CLOWNS

They all wear baggy trousers, t-shirts and funny hats, and wear clown's make-up. Make up your face as shown. Each clown has beanbags for juggling, party whistles and anything else you can find to fool around with.

THE CLOWNS' MAKE-UP

1 Cover your face with white face paint. Use only proper theatrical face paint or make-up.

2 Paint on a big red smile, leaving your lips white. Paint on big black eyebrows.

3 Paint on a bright red nose.

THE BALLERINAS and MUSICIANS

The ballerinas wear tutus and ballet shoes. The musicians wear black trousers with white shirts and black bow ties. Cut the instruments out of stiff cardboard and paint them.

THE DOCTOR

He wears a white shirt and tie and carries a clipboard and pen. Any other props you have, like a briefcase or a thermometer will look good.

BEAUTY'S MIRROR

1 Cut a circle about 50cm across out of cardboard. Cut another circle out of the middle so you can see right through the mirror.

2 Cover the circle in foil.

3 Turn a shoebox upside down and cut a slit along the top and down the sides to a depth of 2.5cm.

4 Paint it silver and slot the mirror into the slit. Put the mirror on the table.

TREASURE CHEST

1 Paint a large cardboard box brown and attach a cardboard lid to it with masking tape.

2 Use a black marker pen to make the tape look like hinges.

3 Make holes in both sides and thread string through them for the handles. Knot the string on the inside.

4 Fill the chest with clothes, shoes and jewellery.

TERRACE WALL

1 Paint several cardboard boxes to look like stone.

2 Line them up to make a terrace wall.

3 Paint flowers and leaves on cardboard, with a wide tab on the bottom of each one. Cut out the shapes. Bend back the tabs and stick the flowers and leaves to the top of the wall so they stand up. Alternatively, cut small slits in the top of the wall and push the tabs through instead of bending them.

ACTS ONE and THREE

These take place in the Merchant's house.

- Make a painting and hang it at the back of the stage.
- Place an armchair, chairs and a table on the stage.
- Put the table and one chair on the right side of the stage. This is Beauty's dressing-table.
- Find or make a bench and place it on the left side of the stage.
- Make a mirror.
- Make a treasure chest for John Paul to carry on-stage.

ACT TWO

This takes place inside the Beast's castle.

- Make flats (see page 6) and paint them grey like a stone wall.
- Turn the painting over to show the sign (below). Hang it from the flats.

ACT FOUR

This takes place on the castle terrace.

- Keep the flats and the bench.
- Make a terrace wall. Place it between the flats and the bench.

BENCH

Use an ordinary bench, or a strong plank of wood placed across two wooden boxes.

PAINTING/SIGN

1 Take a large piece of card and stick a picture on one side.

2 On the other side, write 'Beauty's Chamber' in large letters.

3 Punch two holes in the top and knot a string through the holes.

Beauty's Chamber

THE PLAY
ACT ONE

The Merchant's house. Beauty is reading in an armchair. Her sister Annette is eating chocolates at the table and her brother John Paul is polishing his boots.

Beauty: I'm worried about Father. He should've been back days ago.

Annette: I'm not. It takes time to buy all the presents he promised.

John Paul: He's bringing me shiny new boots. I'll have the best in the village.

Annette: They won't notice your stupid old boots. They'll be too busy admiring my beautiful dresses.

Beauty: I don't care about the presents. I just hope he's safe.

Annette: Of course you don't care about the presents, Beauty. All you asked for was a silly rose.

Beauty: I didn't need anything.

(SOUND) There is a heavy knock at the door. They rush to open the door.

Beauty: Father!

The Merchant ENTERS looking tired. They help him to sit down in the armchair.

Beauty: Thank goodness you're home. I was so worried.

Annette:	Where are the presents? Did you leave them outside?
Merchant:	*(sadly)* There are no presents.
Annette:	What?
John Paul:	Oh, you mean they're coming later.
Annette:	With new servants? I've always wanted my own servant.
Merchant:	There are no presents and no servants. My ships were lost at sea and now we have no money.
Annette:	*(stamping her foot)* How could you? You promised me a hundred new dresses.
Beauty:	Never mind, Father. You're safe. That's all that matters.
Merchant:	I'm afraid there's something worse.
John Paul:	How could there be anything worse? Now I'm going to have to polish these old boots every day.
Merchant:	On my way home I stopped at a castle to rest.
Annette:	I've told all my friends I was getting a hundred new dresses.
Beauty:	Sshh! Go on, Father.
Merchant:	There was a warm fire and a hot meal, and as I was leaving I noticed a beautiful rose bush by the gate. So I picked a rose for Beauty. No sooner had I tucked it in my jacket than a fearsome beast knocked me from my horse.
Beauty:	Oh no. Were you hurt?
Merchant:	No. *(sadly)* But he told me I would have to repay him.

Annette:	*(to Beauty)* See what you've done with your silly rose? Not only do we have no money, but we're in debt, too.
Merchant:	*(shaking his head)* He wouldn't accept money. He said . . . he said . . . *(He puts his head in his hands.)*
Beauty:	What is it, Father?
Merchant:	He said I had to live in the castle for ever, away from my family. He only let me come home to say goodbye to you.
Annette:	He can't do that. Who will pay for our food and clothes?
Merchant:	You'll have to work, I'm afraid.
John Paul:	Work? I can't work. I'm too busy.
Annette:	It's Beauty who should go. She got you into this mess.
John Paul:	That's right. She should be punished. Not us.
Merchant:	No, I can't send Beauty. He's a horrible, fearsome beast.
Beauty:	Annette and John Paul are right. I'm the one who asked for the rose. It's only fair that I should go in your place.
Annette:	Can I have Beauty's room? It's much nicer than mine.
Beauty:	I'll pack my bag.
Merchant:	No. Please, Beauty, you can't.
Beauty:	Father, my mind's made up. *(She EXITS.)*

CURTAIN

ACT TWO

The Beast's castle. The Beast ENTERS RIGHT and Beauty follows him, carrying her suitcase.

Beast: *(growling)* This is your room.

Beauty: *(sadly)* Thank you.

Beast: *(angrily)* You don't like it?

Beauty: *(backing away)* Yes, I do. It's very nice.

Beast: *(walking to the dressing table)* This is a magic mirror. If there's anything that you wish for, just ask the mirror and it will give it to you.

Beauty: Thank you.

Beast: *(growling)* Goodnight.

He EXITS and Beauty sits at the dressing table.

Beauty: *(sighing)* I wish I could see my family.

Annette, John Paul and the Merchant ENTER LEFT. John Paul is carrying a large chest filled with dresses and jewellery. They open the chest and look inside, and take one or two things out.

John Paul: Why would the Beast send all these gifts to us?

Annette: Well, it's only fair, after all the trouble Beauty has caused.

Merchant: *(sadly)* I should have gone in her place.

John Paul: You should have let me go. I'd have shown that Beast a thing or two. *(He pretends to punch the Beast.)*

Annette: Let's go and see what else he sent.

They EXIT LEFT, carrying the chest. (SOUND) There is a knock at the door and the Beast ENTERS RIGHT.

Beast: I've brought you some gifts. A new dress.
A diamond necklace and flowers.
(*Beauty doesn't look up.*)

Beauty: (*sadly*) Thank you.

Beast: (*angry*) You think I'm very ugly don't you?

Beauty: You've been very kind.

Beast: But would you marry me?

Beauty: (*shocked*) Oh, no. I couldn't marry you.

Beast: (*growling*) I thought so.

He EXITS RIGHT. Beauty looks at the mirror again and sighs.

Beauty: Oh, magic mirror I'm so lonely and unhappy.

*Ballerina, a clown, and a musician ENTER LEFT and begin to entertain her.
She laughs and claps her hands. One by one they EXIT LEFT.
(SOUND) There is a knock at the door and the Beast ENTERS RIGHT.
He carries a tray of food to the table.*

Beast: (*shyly*) I've prepared a meal for you. (*He pulls
off the napkin that covers the bowl.*) Your favourites.

Beauty: Thank you. (*She takes a bite.*) Delicious!

Beast: (*proudly*) I've been studying what you like.

Beauty: (*touching his arm*) You've been very kind.

Beast: But would you marry me?

Beauty: (*shaking her head*) No. I couldn't do that.

The Beast sadly EXITS RIGHT.

Beauty: Magic mirror. I'd like to see my father again.

*Annette and John Paul ENTER LEFT and help their father to the bench,
where he lies down. A doctor ENTERS LEFT, takes the
Merchant's pulse, shakes his
head and EXITS LEFT.*

Merchant: (*weakly*) Beauty? Where's Beauty?

Annette: This is Beauty's fault. He's been sick with grief since she left.

John Paul: She's been living in luxury all this time and what do we have?

Annette: That selfish old Beast hasn't sent us a present for ages.

Merchant: (*weakly*) Beauty? Where's Beauty?

Annette: John Paul, help me get Father back into bed.

They help the Merchant up and they EXIT LEFT.

John Paul: It's not fair. We should have servants to do this.

Beauty: (*crying*) Oh poor, poor Father.

(SOUND) There is a knock at the door and the Beast ENTERS RIGHT. He is carrying a stack of books. Beauty dries her eyes with a handkerchief.

Beast: I had to search high and low for these. (*He hands Beauty the books.*) You said you liked books.

Beauty: (*sadly*) I do. Thank you.

Beast: (*clearing his throat*) Beauty, I've tried to give you whatever you wished for since you've been here.

Beauty: Oh yes. You've been very generous.

Beast: But you still find me ugly and hideous.

Beauty:	Not any more. I can see you have a kind and gentle heart.
Beast:	Oh Beauty, could you find it in your heart to marry me?
Beauty:	I'm sorry, Beast. I'm still so sad.
Beast:	But haven't I done everything to make your life happy?
Beauty:	Yes, it's just that – (*She starts to cry.*)
Beast:	Beauty, what have I done?
Beauty:	It's just that my father is ill. He needs me. Please, won't you let me go to him? Just once?

The Beast turns his back on Beauty and thinks, then turns back to her.

Beast:	Very well. But if you stay longer than a week . . . I will die.

Beauty: (*excited*) Oh, thank you. I promise I'll be back. (*She hugs the Beast and EXITS RIGHT.*)

CURTAIN

ACT THREE

The Merchant's house. Beauty is packing her suitcase. Annette and John Paul ENTER and watch her.

Annette:	It's not fair. The Beast gives her all the dresses she wants. And jewels. Anything her heart desires.
John Paul:	Yeah. All we got was one measly trunk of presents.
Annette:	I heard her tell father she had to go back today or the Beast would die.
John Paul:	If the beast died –
Annette:	Then Beauty would be alone.
John Paul:	And I bet we could move into his castle.
Annette:	And all those treasures would be ours. (*Nudging John Paul.*) I have a plan.

They walk over to Beauty.

Annette:	Beauty, why do you have to go today? We've missed you. (*She nudges John Paul.*)
John Paul:	Oh, yeah – and besides, Father needs you.
Annette:	Couldn't you stay just a few more days?
Beauty:	Well I don't know. The Beast needs me.
John Paul:	The Beast? He's a horrible monster.
Beauty:	No, he's not. He's very kind.
Annette:	Poor Father will probably be worse after you've gone.
John Paul:	That's right. I think you should stay to make sure he's completely well.
Beauty:	(*thinking*) Maybe you're right. I should think of Father's health. I'm sure the Beast won't miss me for just a few days.

She picks up her suitcase and EXITS. Annette and John Paul shake hands and EXIT.

CURTAIN

ACT FOUR

The Beast's castle. The Beast is lying on the terrace with his back to the audience. Beauty ENTERS.

Beauty:	Hello, Beast? I'm sorry I'm late. Beast? Where are you? (*She sees the Beast on the floor and runs to him.*) Oh, Beast what have I done? Please don't die. I was unhappy before, but I'm glad to be back. I missed you, Beast. I came back to tell you, dear Beast, that I will gladly marry you.

She puts her head in her hands and starts to cry. The Beast stands up very slowly, keeping his back to the audience. Beauty looks up at him.

Beauty: Beast?

He turns around and the mask is gone. He is a handsome prince.

Beauty: (*surprised*) Who are you?

Beast: Beauty, I'm surprised. Don't you recognise your own Beast?

Beauty: (*standing up*) But how? Why?

The Beast takes her hands and they sit on the bench.

Beast: Many years ago a wicked witch put a spell on me and made me into a hideous monster. The only thing that could save me was for a kind-hearted girl to love me in spite of my ugliness.

Beauty: Why didn't you tell me?

Beast: The spell couldn't be broken if I told you. Do you still want to marry me?

Beauty: Of course! You're still my Beast, no matter what you look like.

The Beast stands and takes Beauty's hand.

Beast: Welcome home, Beauty.

Hand in hand they EXIT.

CURTAIN

ALADDIN
THE STORY

Before the first rehearsal, read through the script on your own so that you know the story. If you are acting a part, think about the character of the person you play and the best way of showing it.

Act 1

An evil magician tricks a young boy, Aladdin, into bringing him a lamp from inside a cave. Aladdin refuses to give it to him, so the magician traps him in the cave. Aladdin rubs the lamp, hoping for some light, but instead a genie appears and helps him to escape.

Act 2

Back home, Aladdin introduces his mother to the genie, who conjures treasure and trays of food for her. Aladdin also tells her a secret – he is in love with Princess Bali, the Sultan's daughter, and he hopes she will agree to marry him, now that he is rich.

THE GENIE
A good-natured genie who must obey the master of the lamp. He enjoys granting Aladdin's wishes.

ALADDIN
An adventurous and brave boy who is quick with ideas, and generous with his new-found wealth.

THE MAGICIAN
A wicked sorcerer, who thinks only of himself and would do anything to be rich.

CAST LIST

- ★ Aladdin
- ★ The Magician
- ★ The Genie
- ★ Aladdin's mother
- ★ Princess Bali
- ★ The Sultan
- ★ Prison guards
- ★ Servants

Act 3

A few days before the wedding, Aladdin takes Princess Bali and her father, the Sultan, to meet his mother. The Sultan, Aladdin and his mother go off to plan the wedding. While the princess is alone, the evil magician comes by and tricks her into giving him the magic lamp.

Act 4

Aladdin finds that the princess, his lamp, and the palace are missing. The magician returns to gloat over what he has done. Aladdin and his mother pour a sleeping powder into the magician's tea, and trick him into drinking it. When he falls asleep, they take the lamp and bring back the princess and the palace. The evil magician is banished to the salt mines.

ALADDIN'S MOTHER
Loves her son very much, although she thinks he is sometimes lazy and mischievous. She is keen to help Aladdin beat the magician.

PRINCESS BALI
A beautiful princess who loves Aladdin not because he is rich but because he is kind and generous.

THE SULTAN
A powerful but kind man who loves his daughter and the people of his kingdom. His greatest pleasure is to see that his daughter is happy.

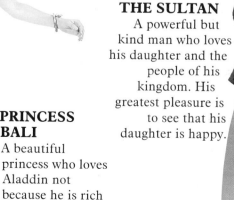

ALADDIN

He wears baggy trousers and a waistcoat with a sash tied around his waist. He also needs a magic lamp. Use a small brass watering can, or paint an old teapot gold. Make the waistcoat as shown.

ALADDIN'S WAISTCOAT

1 Take a piece of felt big enough to reach from your neck to your waist, and to wrap around you.

2 Cut holes for the neck and arms. Sew at the shoulders.

3 Cut slits for the button-holes and sew on buttons.

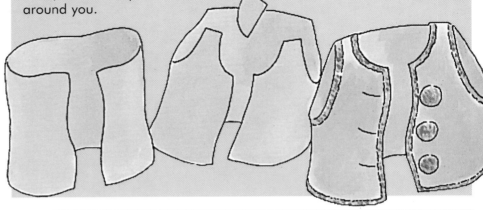

THE MAGICIAN

He wears pyjama bottoms, a shirt, and a black cape that touches the floor. He needs a wheelbarrow full of lamps like Aladdin's, a map of the cave, and a piece of paper for his list of evil deeds. He also needs special make-up, as shown. To make a cape, follow the instructions on page 10.

THE MAGICIAN'S MAKE-UP

1 Paint your face green. Use only proper theatrical face paints or make-up.

2 Paint the outline of a black mask above your eyes, then fill it in with more black.

3 Paint a long black moustache under your nose and down each side of your mouth.

THE GENIE

He wears baggy trousers, a sash, a shirt and a waistcoat. He has a pointed hat, bangles and big earrings. He also needs make-up, as shown. Make the waistcoat as shown above and stick on some glitter with clear glue. To make the hat, cut a large quarter circle out of thin card. Overlap the edges to form a cone, glue together, and decorate with glitter and a tassle.

THE GENIE'S MAKE-UP

1 Paint your face with light blue face paint. Use only proper theatrical face paints or make-up.

2 Paint on a mask around the eyes, nose and mouth in dark blue.

3 Add sparkle with some glitter gel.

THE SULTAN

The Sultan wears pyjama bottoms, a white shirt, a sash round his waist and a turban on his head. Make the turban as shown.

THE SULTAN'S TURBAN

1 Take a large piece of material and wrap it around your head from back to front.

2 Twist the ends at the front and flip them over to the back of your head. Tuck them in and fasten with a safety-pin.

3 Decorate it with 'jewels', which you can make yourself out of painted buttons or gold shapes cut out of foil.

ALADDIN'S MOTHER

She wears a dress with a sash around her waist and carries a pouch for the sleeping powder. She also needs a duster, a broom, a pile of paper/plastic plates, a teapot and three paper/plastic cups. Make the dress and the pouch as shown.

MOTHER'S DRESS AND PURSE

1 Fold a long piece of material in half, and sew or use fabric glue to stick the sides, leaving room for the arms. Cut holes for the neck and arms.

2 Cut a circle of felt and use a paper hole-punch to make holes around the edge.

3 Thread a ribbon through the holes and draw them tight.

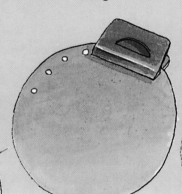
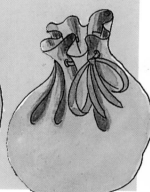

PRINCESS BALI

She wears silky trousers, a t-shirt, a waistcoat and a scarf in her hair. She wears lots of jewellery. To make the waistcoat, follow the instructions on page 38. Decorate it with gold braid or buttons, glued on. Attach a scarf to her hair with hair clips and pin a decorative ornament at the top.

THE PRISON GUARDS

wear pyjama bottoms and t-shirts tied with a sash. They carry swords, which you can cut out from stiff cardboard and cover with foil or paint.

THE SERVANTS

wear pyjama bottoms, and t-shirts tied with a sash. They also wear silver bangles. Each servant needs a tray of food, and another tray piled with treasure. Use silver spoons and dishes, jewellery and ornaments. Don't use anything that is valuable or that might break!

ACT ONE
This is set in and around the cave.

- Make a set of flats (see page 6) and paint them grey like a stone wall.
- Make a cave entrance.
- Make treasure chests to go in the cave.

ACTS TWO, THREE AND FOUR
These are set in Aladdin's house.

- Put a table and some chairs on stage.
- Make a bed by covering two benches with a sheet, or use a mattress.
- In Act Four, put a teapot and cups and saucers on the table.

CAVE ENTRANCE
1 Paint some cardboard boxes to look like stone.
2 Pile them up to make a wall and doorway. Set them diagonally across the stage, so you can see Aladdin when he goes inside.
3 Use the biggest box to cover the entrance, and attach a long string to it. When the Genie makes the stone move, one of the stage crew off-stage pulls the string to move the box away from the cave entrance.

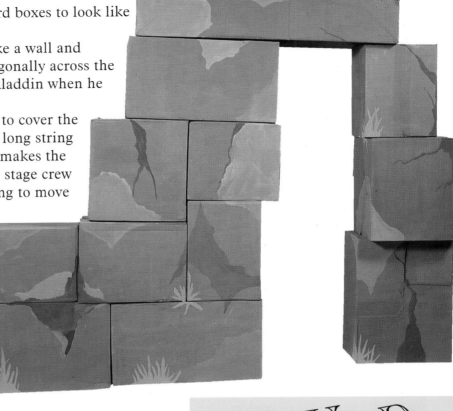

TREASURE CHEST
Make a treasure chest as shown on page 26. Fill it wih clothes, shoes and jewellery.

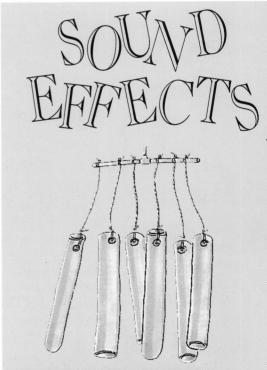

SOUND EFFECTS

THE SOUND OF THE GENIE
Every time the Genie appears or grants a wish, ring a bell or dangle some wind chimes, to make a magical sound.

THE PLAY
ACT ONE

Outside the cave. Aladdin and the Magician ENTER. The Magician is reading a map and taking giant steps towards the cave as he walks.

Magician: *(stopping outside the cave)* Aha! I told you it was here.

Aladdin: It's just a cave. I thought you said it was special.

Magician: *(putting his arm around Aladdin)* It is! It's filled with riches. Gold and diamonds.

Aladdin: Well, what are we waiting for?

Aladdin pulls the Magician towards the cave, but the old man pulls him back.

Magician: Only you can go in, Aladdin.

Aladdin: Great.

He starts to go in, but the Magician pulls him back again.

Magician: But first you must bring me a lamp.

Aladdin: A lamp? A plain old lamp? With all that treasure?

Magician: Bring me the lamp, then you can have whatever you want.

Aladdin: Sure. I can do that. *(They both push a large stone from the entrance and Aladdin goes in.)*

Aladdin: Wow! Look at this! *(He goes to each box and looks through the treasure inside.)*

Magician: *(calling from outside)* Aladdin. Where are you? Have you found the lamp yet?

Aladdin: Oh yeah, I forgot. *(He finds the lamp and bends down to go back through the entrance.)*

Aladdin: Hey. I'm stuck. Help me through.

Magician: First give me the lamp.

Aladdin: Help me through and then I'll give you the lamp.

Magician: *(losing his temper)* Give me that lamp. It's mine.

Aladdin: Well, you're not getting it until you help me out.

Magician: *(yelling)* Aargh! All right then. Stay in there. I'll get another boy to help me. *(He pushes the stone back over the entrance and EXITS.)*

Aladdin: Hey! Hey, what are you doing? Let me out of here. *(He sits down in the middle of all the treasure.)* Now what do I do? It's very dark in here. I wonder if there's any oil in this lamp? *(He shakes the lamp and listens, then rubs it.)* If I could just get this to light.

(SOUND) There is the sound of bells and the Genie leaps up from behind the treasure.

Genie: *(in a booming voice)* I am the Genie of the lamp. What do you require?

Aladdin: *(frightened)* I just wanted some light so that I could see.

Genie: *(crossing his arms)* Your wish is my command. Do you want a hundred torches or a crystal chandelier?

Aladdin: What I'd really like is to get out of here. Can you do that?

Genie: Of course I can. I'm a genie. But are you sure you wouldn't like a chandelier? Lighting is my speciality.

Aladdin: Maybe later.

Genie: *(crossing his arms)* Your wish is my command.

(SOUND) The bells ring as the stone is pulled from the entrance. Aladdin and the Genie go through to the other side.

Aladdin:	Can you give me anything I want?
Genie:	You are the master of the lamp. Your wish is my command.
Aladdin:	(*stretching and yawning*) I'm too tired to think of wishes right now. I just want to go home.
Genie:	Your wish . . .
Aladdin:	I know, I know. But I think I'd rather walk.

They both EXIT.

CURTAIN

ACT TWO

Aladdin's home. Aladdin is asleep on his bed. The lamp is on the floor beside him. His mother ENTERS RIGHT with a duster and broom.

Mother:	Sleeping late again, Aladdin?

Aladdin groans and rolls over in his bed.

Mother:	(*picking up the lamp*) And still bringing home junk from the market, I see. Look at this. It's filthy.

She rubs the lamp with her dust cloth. (SOUND) The sound of bells and the Genie pops up from behind the bed.

Genie:	Your wish is my command.

Aladdin's mother screams. She picks up a broom to protect herself.

Aladdin:	(*leaping from bed*) It's all right, Mother. It's just the Genie of the lamp. He's come to live with us.
Mother:	Live with us? And what do you think we're going to feed him? We hardly have enough for ourselves.
Aladdin:	He doesn't need food. He can give us whatever we want. Watch this. Genie?

Genie: Yes, master?

Aladdin: My mother would like a feast fit for a queen.

Genie: Your wish is my command.

(SOUND) The sound of bells as several servants ENTER carrying trays piled high with fruit and vegetables. They put the trays on the table, then EXIT.

Mother: Oh, my! All this for me?

Aladdin: Yes, and that's not all. Genie? Bring me treasure fit for a Sultan.

Genie: Your wish is my command.

(SOUND) The sound of bells and the servants ENTER LEFT with treasure. They put it on the floor and EXIT LEFT.

Mother: Oh, Aladdin. We're rich.

Aladdin: Yes, we are. *(He sighs.)* But there's only one thing I really want.

Genie: Oh, goodie. I was hoping you'd let me do some decorating. You could really use some new curtains. Pure silk. What do you think?

Mother: And what's wrong with my house? I'll have you know, we have a very nice house.

Aladdin: I don't want curtains, Genie. I want to marry Princess Bali.

Mother: Are you crazy? The Sultan will never allow you to marry his daughter.

Aladdin: He will now that I'm rich. *(He picks up a tray of treasure and holds it up then EXITS RIGHT.)*

CURTAIN

ACT THREE

Aladdin's home. Aladdin ENTERS LEFT with Princess Bali and the Sultan.

Aladdin: Mother. We're here.

Mother ENTERS RIGHT.

Aladdin: Mother, this is the Sultan and his daughter, Princess Bali.

Mother: *(bowing)* Welcome to my home, great Sultan.

Sultan: I am very pleased to meet the mother of my future son-in-law.

Princess Bali: You must be very proud of your son. He's always helping others and giving gold to the poor.

Sultan: Aladdin built a magnificent palace for me. The finest I've ever seen. (*He looks around the stage.*) You should ask Aladdin for a palace of your own.

Mother: *(crossing her arms)* There's nothing wrong with my house. I like it the way it is.

Princess Bali: Would you like to help with the wedding? Aladdin has invited everyone in the village.

Sultan: It will be a magnificent affair.

Mother: We should have a special meal to celebrate the wedding. I'll be right back.
(*She EXITS RIGHT.*)

Sultan: *(to Aladdin.)* Now then. Should we have camels or stallions for the wedding procession?

The Sultan and Aladdin walk off-stage LEFT. A few seconds later the Magician ENTERS LEFT pushing a wheelbarrow filled with lamps. He stands at the corner of the stage.

Magician:	New lamps for old. New lamps for old.
Princess Bali:	Excuse me, sir. Did you say you would give a brand new lamp for an old one?
Magician:	That's right. Sparkling new ones for old rusty ones.
Princess Bali:	That would be a nice surprise for Aladdin. *(She picks up Aladdin's lamp and gives it to the Magician.)*
Magician:	Thank you, my dear. *(He hands her the new lamp and EXITS LEFT.)*
Princess Bali:	It's so shiny and new. I can't wait to show Aladdin. *(She runs off stage LEFT.)* Aladdin! Aladdin! I have a surprise for you.

ACT FOUR

Aladdin's home. Aladdin's mother is sitting alone. Aladdin ENTERS LEFT.

Aladdin:	*(very worried)* Is Princess Bali here?
Mother:	No one is here. I work hard all day making a special meal and when I bring it out, what do I find? An empty house.
Aladdin:	*(sitting at the table and putting his head in his hands.)* Oh no. Oh no.
Mother:	Aladdin? What's wrong?
Aladdin:	Princess Bali has disappeared and the palace I built for the Sultan is gone. It vanished before our very eyes. *(He looks up.)* The Genie can help me. The lamp. Where is my lamp? *(He looks around and looks at his mother.)*
Mother:	*(shrugging)* I don't have it.

The Magician ENTERS LEFT. He holds the lamp up.

Magician:	Is this what you're looking for?
Aladdin:	How did you get my lamp?

Aladdin reaches for it but the Magician pulls it away.

Magician:	It's my lamp now. I tricked your little princess into giving it to me.

Aladdin:	What have you done with her?
Magician:	Oh she's safe and sound. She's living in your precious palace, thousands of miles away, in the desert. Which is where I'm sending you and the Sultan. And I'll be ruler then. *(He dances around laughing and singing.)* I'll be ruler then . . . I'll be ruler then . . .
Aladdin:	*(to his mother)* We have to stop him.
Mother:	*(holding up a small pouch)* Sleeping powder?
Aladdin:	Yes of course. *(to the Magician)* Before you send me to the desert, would you allow me one last cup of tea with my mother?
Magician:	Oh, all right. But make it quick. I have a hundred evil deeds to do today. *(He checks his list.)* Let's see. 'Outlaw puppies.' Check. 'Take food from the orphanage.' Check.

While he is going over his list, Mother pours the tea. Aladdin pours the sleeping powder into one cup and keeps it for himself.

Mother:	*(offering him another cup)* Won't you join us? It's my special blend.
Magician:	*(walking towards them)* I am a little dry with all this work. *(He stops.)* Wait a minute – I know what you're doing. I'll have your tea. *(He grabs Aladdin's cup and gulps it down.)* Thought you could fool me didn't you? *(His words slow down as he slumps to the floor.)* Well I'm . . . the . . . greatest . . . Magician . . . *(He snores.)*

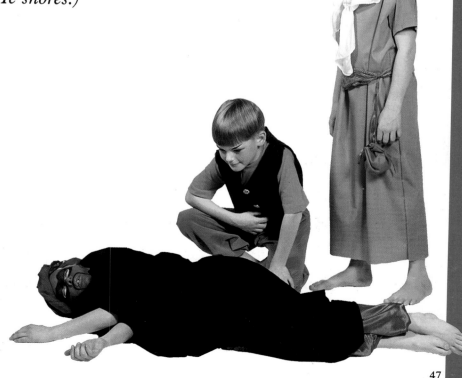

Mother: It worked!

Aladdin takes the lamp and rubs it. (SOUND) The sound of bells as the Genie ENTERS LEFT.

Genie: *(sadly)* I am the Genie of the lamp. What do you require? *(He sees Aladdin and cheers up.)* Oh, it's you!

Aladdin: Welcome back. And now my first command. Bring Princess Bali safely home.

Genie: Your wish is my command.

(SOUND) The sound of bells as the Sultan and the Princess ENTER LEFT. The Princess runs to Aladdin.

Mother: *(pointing off-stage LEFT)* Aladdin! Look! The palace is back, too.

Aladdin: *(to the Genie)* Now send this man to work in the salt mines.

Genie: My pleasure. I mean – your wish is my command.

(SOUND) The sound of bells as two prison guards ENTER LEFT and take the Magician away.

Sultan: I think we should prepare for the wedding.

Aladdin, Princess Bali and the Sultan EXIT LEFT. Mother tugs on the Genie's sleeve.

Mother: Now that you're back, do you think I could have those silk curtains and a Persian rug?

Genie: *(smiling)* Your wish is my command.

CURTAIN